This book is dedicated to each of my patients and to all the children of this amazing planet. You deserve to know the truth of who you really are.

-Dr. Jill Garripoli Pedalino

The Universe Is Listening

Written by
Dr. Jill Garripoli Pedalino

Illustrated by
Lina Safar

What is the Universe anyway?

It is the energy all around us and it is filled with every possibility we can imagine!

We cannot hear it or touch it...

We cannot taste it, smell it, or even see it...

But, we CAN feel it!

The Universe communicates with us through our feelings. It's our own built-in guidance system! How we feel can tell us if we are allowing the Universe to bring us happiness or not.

Did you know that
the Universe is always listening
and waiting to hear
your next thought?

It is waiting to hear your next desire,
your next big idea,
and your next dream
for yourself.

You see, the Universe understands that
you are a very powerful creator
and it is waiting to hear your next thought that
makes you excited about life!

The Universe is also
listening to the worries
and the doubts
that you think
when you are scared
or sad.

Did you know that the Universe has a secret?

The secret is that the Universe will ALWAYS give you whatever it is that you think about.

If you want to be happier than you are right now, but you keep thinking about how unhappy you are then the Universe will keep giving you more things to be unhappy about!

When you think about wanting more happiness and then find little things that make you happy the Universe will keep leading you toward more happiness!

It can be easy to forget how powerful your thoughts are so you have to be VERY careful about what you choose to think.

Another secret of the Universe is that your body is listening to your thoughts, too!

Your thoughts are so powerful that happy and positive thoughts can make your heart feel excited and you can feel stronger and healthier and you have more energy!

But, sad or scared or negative thoughts can make your stomach hurt and give you a headache and you will feel like you don't have much energy at all.

You are so very powerful that you can actually decide which thoughts you want to think that will create that feeling in your body!

Doesn't it feel so much better to think happier thoughts and then watch your body feel and look happier, healthier, and stronger?

It does not matter if you are young or old, short or tall, big or small...

It does not matter where you are from,
how many things you own, or the color of
your eyes, your skin, or your hair...

What matters most is that you never forget that only YOU can control the way you think and you can create your own happiness.

The Universe can't wait to bring you all the wonderful things that make you feel full of happiness and love and joy!

Remember, the Universe is always listening,

so go ahead and try it out!

You will see how powerful you really are!

About the Author

Dr. Jill Garripoli Pedalino is an award-winning Pediatrician and owner of Healthy Kids Pediatrics in New Jersey.

While pursuing her Bachelor of Arts Degree in English and Biology and graduating with honors from Bucknell University, she enjoyed breaking a few bones (including a few of her own) as captain of the women's rugby team. She obtained her degree in Osteopathic Medicine from the University of Medicine and Dentistry of New Jersey and completed her pediatric specialty training at Robert Wood Johnson University Hospital.

"Dr. Jill," as she is affectionately called by her patients, has been voted one of New Jersey's Top Docs and Favorite Kids' Docs by NJ Family Magazine for the past 10 years.

When she's not caring for her patients, posting helpful parenting articles, writing inspirational children's books, or delivering impactful keynote presentations, Dr. Jill enjoys hiking, biking, and kayaking with her family as well as crushing a challenging crossword puzzle with a nice cup of tea at their condo in Costa Rica.

Dr. Jill strives for open communication with parents so together they may guide their children to be the most successful, healthy, and productive adults possible. She works hard to be a role model for her patients and knows she's in the right profession when a parent tells her, "Doctor Jill, you make a difference."